WHAT NOW?

Take Control
Live Life; Don't Let it Live You

Calvin Williams, M.A.

Blue Marble Books, LLC

Publisher   Henry S. Beers
Associate Publisher   Rick L. Nolte
Executive VP   Robert G. Aldrich
Editor-in-Chief   Joni Woolf
Designer   Scott Baber
Print Studio Manager Gary G. Pulliam
Print Studio Assistant Nick Malloy

©2010 Calvin Williams

All rights reserved. No part of this book may be reproduced in any form or by any means without prior written permission from the publisher, except for brief quotations used in reviews written specifically for inclusion in a magazine, newspaper, or broadcast media.

Disclaimer: *Blue Marble Books, LLC does not assume any legal liability or responsibility for the accuracy of any information or content in this publication.*

Library of Congress Control Number: *Data In Process*

ISBN: (13 digit) 978-1-934144-57-2
       (10 digit) 1-934144-57-6

Blue Marble Books are available at quantity discounts with bulk purchase for educational, business, or sales promotional use. For information, please write to: Blue Marble Books, LLC, 7400 Airport Drive, Macon, Georgia 31216, or call 478-788-7171.

DEDICATION

This book is dedicated to my family and friends who had the strength to allow me to be myself and pursue a lifelong dream to write a book. Their selfless approach to life and encouragement provided me with the springboard to conceive this book and additional topics for future publication.

FOREWORD

How do I introduce Calvin Williams? At first my thoughts turn to his professional credentials, but he has experienced so much and enriched the hearts and lives of so many people, those credentials can't describe the real Calvin Williams. After an impressive military career of over 20 years, Calvin began work as a Career Specialist at Macon State College. It is in this capacity that I had the opportunity to observe his keen interest in assisting college students to meet their potential. Calvin is committed to improving quality of life – not only his own but also of those he encounters.

In our dreams we all aspire to greatness. Yet, most of us simply aren't creating the results we want in life. Calvin shares a journey of reflection and exploration in pursuit of his personal and professional goals. He offers the reader a plan of action to change life, an opportunity to make life exciting and rewarding, and an opportunity to discover passion in life. Calvin emphasizes how thoughts and actions are in every aspect of our lives, even in our approach with reading this book. Norman Vincent Peale said, "Change your thoughts and you change the world." Of course, it sounds considerably simpler than it is. Calvin weaves a course of action with positive, progressive thoughts.

Mother Teresa reminds us, "We cannot do great things on this earth. We can only do small things with great love." Calvin has found this to be true. He provides a road map for the reader to seek adventure through local resources, volunteerism, and building meaningful relationships.

This is a book written by a man with a good heart and an indomitable spirit who is willing and eager to share in order to help others. "He is a man who practices what he preaches." This book will help you to understand:

- the mysteries of yourself,
- the miracle of relationship, and
- the magic of living.

Calvin's word will touch your heart, this book can change your life!

Ann Loyd
Director of Counseling
Macon State College

TABLE OF CONTENTS

Introduction	ix
Chapter 1 – Enjoy some time off	1
Chapter 2 – Take a vacation	11
Chapter 3 – Reconnect	23
Chapter 4 – Time for a hobby	35
Chapter 5 – Volunteer	47
Chapter 6 – Teach one, reach one	61
Chapter 7 – Network, network and network some more!	75
Chapter 8 – Go back to school	89
Chapter 9 – Get a Mentor	103
Chapter 10 – Live life	115
Acknowledgements	121

INTRODUCTION

My purpose for this book is not to encourage everyone to go out and quit their jobs today! This book should be viewed as a way to 'work' through the process of being without a job and realize life goes on. For those of you thinking about a life transition, you will find this process can help as you plan your future. Why wait until the last minute? Live life, don't let life live you is a personal statement I have been making for quite some time. It always sounded good and I thought I fully understood my intended purpose for using this motto. I actually had to step away from things in my normal comfort zone to finally see ways to actually live life instead of going through the motions and calling it living.

Getting to this point was an eye opening journey for me and one I wanted to share with others who may be in a similar life pattern or planning a big career change decision. My personal approach to my time off was done in a conscious and deliberate manner. I do not view myself as a victim of circumstance; I believe life happens and we need to have an active hand in planning and living our lives. Having time off from work provides a springboard to explore what is important in our individual lives. Some will discover this is the break in life they have been dreaming about and now they can begin to live a fuller life. Many times we spend more time worrying about the next staff meeting or business trip and forget to truly live our lives. How many working lunches have you spent in the office or missed lunch completely because of a conference call?

This project is not intended to be an autobiographical depiction of life but I have inserted myself into this process to highlight how my journey can be used as a model for others. This is not an attempt to cover everything we can get done in a lifetime but a way to model a mindset change to start living life. Each chapter can be viewed as an individual step in your personal journey as you discover ways to truly live life. Some who read this may find all the chapters listed can be applied to their personal life. You may also discover avenues not listed to apply to your individual life circumstance. Remember to write down the new things you discover so you can explore them fully in the future. Take the chapters and situations which fit you and then map out your plan for your personal journey. The subjects listed are all things that can enrich your life and make you a more interesting person in all aspects of your life. This book is a revelation of sorts of what can be discovered in life while 'experiencing' some downtime from work.

Chapter 1
ENJOY SOME TIME OFF

Yesterday you were working; today you do not have a job! What in the world are you going to do with yourself? Relax, do not panic, the world did not officially end. It may seem like it did because all you have ever known is get up in the morning and head straight to work. While at work, there were always meetings to attend, proposals to make and working lunches you needed to coordinate. You may have found time on occasion to check your email, browse the internet for the latest news and chat with friends and co-workers. You finally get to head home after all that excitement just to hang out in front of the television, computer or catch up on your reading for the rest of the night. The next step is to head to bed so you can start this wonderful process all over again in the morning.

Without a job, a major portion of your day seems to have evaporated right before your eyes. That was my initial viewpoint after I decided it was time for me to leave my job. The decision and process of leaving was well thought out but: What Now?

I spent 20 years in the Air Force working as a data analyst, training instructor and a section chief. After leaving (retiring) the service I took a full 'three' weeks off and went straight back to work because my need to work was so great. I changed work environments two additional times with even smaller amounts of time off between leaving one position and starting another. I was always in a rush to get back in the world of the employed but never gave myself time to adjust or even transition from one experience to the next. My mindset was I needed to get back to work as soon as possible and idle time was wasted time. For me there was not an obvious need or outside interference to rush this process; I just felt or maybe created the urge to get to work as quickly as possible. This seemed like the natural progression or path for me since all I have known in my adult life is to get up and go to work...it is the American way, right?

A more novel approach would be to use time away from work to live a little and find new adventure in your life. Why not give it a try?

Enjoying time away from work takes a little getting used to. There is not a set time to be anywhere during the day so your time belongs to you. Take a few days to sleep in during the week as a reward to yourself.

This will probably be the first time in your adult life you actually get to sleep in on a Wednesday and not have to feel guilty. Do not view this as your official authorization to just lie around the house and worry about the future. Use the opportunity to sleep in as a way to recharge your personal, emotional and professional batteries.

This process was very foreign to me because in the past I was an early riser because I went to the gym to lift weights in the mornings before work. Arriving at the gym at 5 a.m. was a huge part of my daily routine. I would get to work at 7:30 to begin tackling my daily tasks after my workouts. The first two weeks without having to worry about going to work allowed me to practice sleeping in. The positive effects on my psyche and physical makeup this process brought was amazing. After enjoying sleeping in for awhile I made it a point to get and stay in the gym. My daily workout routine has been a major part of my life and I wanted to ensure I took care of myself physically. I decided to create a schedule to ensure I got to the gym and completed my workouts early so I could enjoy the rest of the day.

Most people will get the urge or feel pressure to get back to work as soon as possible. Your life situations will dictate how soon you need to start your efforts to get back into the work environment. Family, financial and life obligations will vary from person to person. You will need to look at these factors when making the decision to enjoy some time away from work. Do not put yourself or your family in a financial bind. If circumstances in your life dictate the need for a steady paycheck right away; then the amount of time between the job loss and the job search will be less than for someone who can 'afford' an extended amount of time off. There is not a cookie cutter approach to any of our lives; if you need to get back to work right away, enjoy a little time off to catch your breath, let your hair down a bit, and then get back to work.

An interesting thing I found with my time away from work was I suddenly had time to have lunch with my friends. Friends discovered I was available to have lunch with them at any time during the day since my schedule was free from work related tasks. No longer was I 'confined' to my prescribed lunch hour; anytime lunch was served fit my schedule just fine. This fact eliminated friends from having to worry about coordinating their prescribed lunch hour with my old 12 – 1 pm lunch hour. Another bonus is I did not have to coordinate with coworkers to ensure there was appropriate office coverage so I could go to lunch at another time.

Being available to do lunch any time during the day made me a very popular lunch request. I was able to reconnect with friends over lunch and did not have to rush back to work or call back to say I was running a little late. Having lunch with friends who work second shifts or who are not working allows plenty of time to sit and catch up over a nice meal. What's the rush? Friends I never had time to have lunch with were now open for business. They could take their regular lunch hours and I fit my day around their availability. It did not matter if they called to let me know they were running late; I had the time. Last minute changes simply meant I had more time out of the house to enjoy the fullness of that particular day.

When was the last time you caught a matinee movie during the week? This is a foreign concept to most people who work throughout the week. Sure we catch matinees on the weekends to save a little money but did you know movie theatres have matinees during the week? The best part of this is during the week (minus summer vacation for the kids) there are no crowds to fight with to catch a movie. Simply walk up to the ticket counter and see the new movie that just came out during matinee hours. No long lines to wait in, no hassles at the concession stand and you have your pick of any seat in the theatre. You can even laugh out loud if you want to, depending on how many people are in the theatre with you.

For those who do not want to go to the movie theatre by themselves you still have the option to leave the house and rent or buy a movie. Most people have their own surround sound system at home so enjoying a movie during the day at home is perfectly acceptable. Pop your own popcorn, get a drink, kick up your feet and enjoy the show. Viewing movies at home will actually let you watch some older movies from your personal collection you have not viewed in some time. I was able to discover numerous John Wayne westerns I had never seen or heard of and quickly added them to my collection of DVDs. This was like finding a pot of gold for me since I am a huge western's movie fan.

Does your city have a museum or cultural district? If it does, then make it a point to enjoy the culture your city presents. Discount prices can be found for museum exhibits during the week which can help keep your costs down. The Sports, Art and Science and African-American museums available to me seemed like obscure entities when I was working. I knew they existed and had a general idea where they were located but never had or made the time to find or enter one. My weekends were filled with more important things and the museums never really fit. Being out of the working environment took away my excuses for not taking in the museums and cultural activities available to me.

A day trip to the museum can be a very enlightening experience. There is a certain peace of mind experienced when viewing art exhibits I never imagined I would get to see. I got a chance to share this experience with my niece, Jayla when she visited me during her spring break. We actually sat down to critique art together and had a ball doing it. This was a very good bonding excursion and we both were able to enjoy the cultural adventure. I was able to experience this quality time first-hand because I did not have to worry about work obligations.

Take the opportunity to stop and get a cup of coffee while you are out. Star Bucks, Barnes and Nobles and Books-A-Million provide areas where you can sit and relax with your favorite beverage. People watching as you enjoy your coffee or use your laptop is a very relaxing way to complete a day after enjoying the museum district. Take a little time to window shop while you are out. Allow your senses to take in your surroundings and let the possibilities around you manifest.

There are numerous things available to fill the void of not getting up in the morning and heading for work. Use the time afforded during your 'break' to get out and enjoy life. The old adage: "Live a little" is staring you squarely in the face, why not try it? This is your chance to "Live life" daily regardless if you are working or not.

ENJOY SOME TIME OFF
(ACTION PLAN)

How can you make this time beneficial for you?

_____
_____
_____
_____
_____
_____

List potential activities to explore during your time off

_____
_____
_____
_____
_____
_____
_____

List friends or family members to contact for lunch

_____
_____
_____
_____
_____
_____

List potential cultural sites to visit in your area

_____
_____
_____
_____
_____
_____

List potential books you would like to read

_____
_____
_____
_____
_____
_____

List your hobbies (real and potential)

_____
_____
_____
_____
_____
_____
_____

What have you always wanted to do but never made the time?

_____
_____
_____
_____
_____
_____

Chapter 2
TAKE A VACATION

This may be the perfect opportunity to take that vacation you never seemed to have time for now that you have some free time on your hands. Similarly how not working frees up time to enjoy lunch with friends, you do not have to 'schedule' your vacation with anyone either. This allows you to take advantage of last minute travel specials or to just decide to get away on an obscure Tuesday for a little rest and relaxation you deserve. Where have you always wanted to go but never actually took the time to make the travel arrangements and go? Well here is your time to see the sights!

Call your travel agent or even book the trip yourself using numerous travel sites (Expedia, Priceline, Travelocity, etc.). Your search can target the least expensive days to travel with any service you use since you are not limited by time constraints. Take off and find a secluded beach to enjoy the sun, surf and find your peace of mind. Look into getting away to the mountains if the beach is not your ideal vacation destination. The point is for you to get out and enjoy life; it does not really matter the type of vacation you take or the specific location. You can get away for a day, a weekend or for an entire week if you like. The key is to enjoy life by living a little differently than you have in the past.

My time away from work was used to book a vacation to my favorite location, Negril, Jamaica. My wife and I have been down there numerous times but our trips were always scheduled during the summer when most people take their vacations. The crowds during this timeframe have never been extreme but there were more people on the island during the summer competing with our fun time. With my time away from work, I decided to look into heading down to Jamaica in January which is considered the off-season in the Caribbean. The prices for a round-trip ticket and resort stay were much more cost effective than they had been when booking during the summer vacation season. My resort of choice even had free on-line upgrades because they had numerous vacancies since this was the off-peak timeframe for vacationers. This was an added bonus and provided even more incentive to book the vacation and get away for a bit. If I did not mention it before, I am a beach person! I really love to get out and enjoy the sights, sand and relaxing atmosphere the beach affords. A day spent snorkeling off the cliffs of Negril beats a good day in the office every time.

My trip started off with a bang because I was able to get a 'free' upgrade to first class on the plane ride down to Jamaica. The plane I was on was half empty since this was the off-season for tourist heading down to Jamaica. All I had to do was ask the head flight attendant if she would mind if I moved to first class to stretch out and I was in! It never hurts to smile and compliment your flight attendant when asking for a free upgrade. The first class section consisted of me and two other people who were already up there enjoying the extra leg room. The process of heading down to Jamaica on vacation helped to take my mind away from not working. In fact, thinking about work or getting back to work did not cross my mind as I ventured further into my much needed vacation. The goal was to enjoy my 'free' time as much as possible.

My time spent in Jamaica consisted of simply enjoying myself on the beach and if you are familiar with Negril, the cliffs on the west end of the island. I did as much or as little as I wanted to, but the premise for the trip was to enjoy life at my own, relaxed pace. Seeking out areas the Jamaicans themselves frequented was something I wanted to do to really enhance my experience and soak in the cultural aspects of the island. I sought out the places and things people from the islands did instead of heading for all the normal tourist outlets and attractions.

I quickly discovered Alfred's, a local favorite hangout was the best place to hear live reggae music on Wednesday nights in Negril. Taxi drivers are a good source of cultural information when asked. The crowd consisted of the locals who came to hear their favorite reggae musicians and tourist like me who were trying to catch an authentic Irie vibe. This unique mix of people created a friendly and relaxed environment to enjoy the live musical sets of the local bands. The reggae music vibe seems to bring the dancer out in everyone even if they do not normally find themselves on a dance floor.

Rick's Café was identified as the best place to watch cliff divers perform their art on a daily basis. Rick's Café has been voted the Caribbean's Best Live Reggae Bar and Caribbean's Best Sunset by Caribbean Travel and Life Magazine. After visiting there I can see why the travel magazines and their editors view this location so favorably. Rick's Café turned out to be an ideal vantage point for me to catch some amazing sunsets which I made a point to take numerous digital photos to bring back with me to share. I have never taken a photo of a sun rise but I am a huge fan of seeing the sun set over the ocean horizon and Rick's Cafe did not disappoint.

What is a trip to Negril, Jamaica without stopping by Jimmy Buffet's Margaritaville? The atmosphere is great and you get a chance to meet people from all over the world who are drawn in by the Margaritaville brand and tunes by Jimmy Buffet. Margaritaville is centrally located on Negril's Seven Mile Beach and provides access to jet skis, catamaran boat trips and a giant water trampoline. You can kick back with your favorite drink and enjoy your tropical Margaritaville experience.

An interesting part of staying at a resort in Negril is the ability to catch a boat directly from your resort. Many Jamaicans make their living on the water and if you are seeking to get from one place to another, the availability of boat captains is unlimited. My favorite boat captain, Eryle, seemed to always be ready and willing to get me from one location to another. All I had to do was stand by the cliffs at the resort and wave when his boat came by and then my daily adventure could start. Most times Eryle and other boat captains were just anchored close by waiting for someone who needed a ride to their favorite destination. Snorkeling or scuba diving is made a lot easier when you can decide when and where you want to go.

The prices provided by these independent boaters is much better than if booked through the resort or a Jamaican travel agency. The independence this type of travel brings is a major advantage when exploring the cliffs and reefs around Negril. You have your own personal boat with an able bodied captain who will deliver you anywhere you want for a very reasonable price. You do not have to rush through your water adventure because you have hired the boat for as long as you need it. You can even request them to drop you off at a location and come back to pick you up at an agreed upon time. You do not have to worry about being stranded; the boat captains take a lot of pride in taking care of their customers. This level of dedication also ensures they get repeat customers to use their boat services. No worries man! Many boat captains provide similar customer satisfaction so you will not be limited in your options to get out on the water and enjoy your time in the Jamaican waters.

The resorts on Negril's west end are all situated on cliffs. This aspect provides another dimension to vacationing in Negril. Cliff diving is a very popular way for many visitors to enjoy their time in Jamaica. People who are not cliff divers can enjoy watching others take their turn going over the cliffs. The resorts provide numerous opportunities to enjoy your time in Jamaica with events and activities. Most have an all-inclusive package which allows visitors to experience Caribbean cuisine and drinks in an all-you-can eat and drink format. This option eliminates having to go from place to place looking for the next meal. The resorts are also an ideal place to find local entertainment at no additional cost. Local musical acts can be heard nightly at many resorts located on Negril's west end. Simply come outside of your room, get an all-inclusive drink or two from the bar and enjoy the music throughout the night.

Taking a cruise is another option you may want to explore for your vacation options. Deals can be found using the same travel sites mentioned when referring to my trip to Jamaica. Decide if a 3-day, 4-day or longer cruise is right for you and then pick a destination. Selecting a destination you have always wanted to visit or heard good things about from friends and family makes this more of an adventure. Cruising can be fun because you can enjoy all on-board ship activities, shore excursions or a combination of both. Some people will never get off their cruise ship while others cannot wait to get to the next port so they can explore and shop. Either way is fine as long as you are selecting the activities that fit your vacation style. You will soon discover you can do as much as you desire or as little as you want while cruising. Sit by the pool with your favorite book and a tropical drink, catch the on-board shows or spend time in the casino trying your luck against the house. Getting a deck level massage or taking yoga classes in the fitness center are other activities you may enjoy on the cruise. Cruising combines several 'little' vacation activities into one big package, the cruise.

The beach or taking a cruise may not be the ideal vacation for everyone. Some may not enjoy attending a concert of their favorite artist in another city. I have always heard how 'Dead Heads' follow the Grateful Dead group from one city to the next. Why not use this concept and turn it into a vacation for yourself? Look up your favorite group or artist to see where they are playing next and then make the travel arrangements to get there to see them. Go out to the venue a few days early and take in the atmosphere of the city and the surrounding areas. Tailgate before the show with the locals and enjoy your experience before, during and after the show.

National parks provide another vacation option while enjoying time away from work. These parks can be seen as day trips or spread out over a week or two if needed. Take time to explore the Great Smokey Mountains or try hiking in Yellowstone national park. Budget friendly outings can be found in numerous locations throughout the country. Identify a location you have always wanted to visit and make the necessary travel arrangements. Since spending money is not the objective; look for parks and locales which fit your current financial situation. Hiking, bike riding and sightseeing excursions should provide plenty opportunities to get out and enjoy nature without having to spend large sums of money in the process.

Take this time away from work as your chance to finally get away from it all. The vacation you have always been 'planning' to take does not have to be put off any longer. A vacation can be used to recharge your mental and physical batteries. This time will also allow you to see life in a different perspective and help tackle your pending job search with added zeal. The available time you have now may disappear again once you start working so why not use your time wisely and get a little vacation time in? This will signify you are actively living and enjoying your life at a maximal level.

TAKE A VACATION
(ACTION PLAN)

Where have you always wanted to go?

_____
_____
_____
_____
_____
_____

When can you start your vacation?
How many days can you spend on vacation?

_____
_____
_____
_____
_____
_____

What vacation type is the best fit for you?

Beach _____

Cruise _____

Mountains _____

Other _____

Who has the best prices for your vacation preference?

Expedia _____

Priceline _____

Hotwire _____

Other _____

Other _____

What activities are available at your preferred vacation destination?

_____

_____

_____

_____

_____

_____

_____

Do you need a passport? Is it current?

CHAPTER 3
RECONNECT

How many times have you promised yourself you were going to stay in better contact with family and friends? Most of us make this statement early each year (think resolution) as a way to make ourselves feel good. The process of actually making this happen seems to get away from us each year. We have good reasons and intentions when we make this declaration but most of us are lacking in our follow through. Why not use this time to really get connected with your family and friends?

The time you have away from work provides the opportunity to catch up with family members and friends. You can choose to reconnect in person, email, text message or telephone. The method you choose is not the important thing; just pick the most convenient way you can to reach out in your effort to reconnect. You are available now to sit down with family and friends for extended visits without the need to rush through a cursory visit. Relatives who do not live close by provide a perfect excuse to take a road trip or book a flight for a visit. You may want to make sure the relatives you plan to visit know you are coming before just dropping in on them! You can ensure the quality of the visit is maintained because you do not have work obligations to rush back home for. Have lunch with mom or dad at a place of their choice; relax and enjoy the time you have together. They may actually be surprised when you suggest going out to lunch together especially if this is something you have never done before. Try picking up a takeout lunch and bringing it with you if your parents do not want to go out for lunch. The quality time you seek can be enjoyed in any setting; it does not have to be a fancy restaurant or bistro.

Lunch is a perfect opportunity to catch up with family or friends you have not talked to in awhile. We mentioned in Chapter 1 the benefits you 'gained' by not having to rush back to work or being limited by a set lunch hour. You can simply let them know you are available and can meet them at a time convenient for them to fit their schedules. How many times have you said to a family member or friend, "Hey, let's do lunch sometime"? That time never seemed to arrive because both of you were always too busy to actually schedule and go to lunch. Well, now you have time on your hands and you are available. Make the call and start to reconnect with your family and friends.

Coffee shops and book stores are other options to explore when trying to reconnect with people in your life. These places provide an atmosphere which allows you to carry on conversations without being interrupted by others. You can spread out and enjoy your companions in a location which is convenient for both of you. Most of these venues have comfortable chairs and sofas just like your living room or den. Stake out your spot, get your favorite beverage and sit back and enjoy the time together as you catch up on life. You will be amazed how quickly life moves and the things you may have missed because you never had or made time to sit down and connect with family and friends in this manner.

Picking up the phone and starting a conversation will also provide a good way to reconnect with family and friends. Most of us have home and cell phones so you will have to decide which fits your calling preferences. I am sure your family and friends would have a problem if you started using up their anytime minutes now that you are not working. They know you have a lot of free time but if they are like my family and friends, anytime minutes are treated like gold and they do not want them wasted even if I am trying to catch up with them. They may appreciate a call to their home phone during the day to avoid using up their cell phone minutes. Make the call regardless of which format you decide to use.

You do not have to rehash everything from your past but this is your attempt to 'catch up' with family and friends. Let them know what is new in your life and find out how they are doing. My mother has five brothers and four sisters so I have a lot of family members to stay in contact with. A simple five minute call may be a springboard to a very good conversation with a cousin you have not seen or talked with in awhile. This is a good time to see how they are doing in life, at work, in school and on a personal level.

Using this approach allowed me to reconnect and visit with one of my cousins I had not seen in over 18 years. My constant relocating while serving in the Air Force was a major reason we lost touch initially. Turns out she moved to Athens, Georgia from Maryland a few years back and actually lives about two hours from me now. We have been able to sit down to begin the process of catching up on the years we lost contact. We both have standing invitations to visit each other whenever we want and plan to stay in contact better than we had in the past.

Has your family always talked about having a family reunion but there are never any volunteers to actually plan and organize the event? Well, with the time you currently have away from work, you may be the perfect candidate to plan a family reunion and help the entire family in the process. Your personal efforts to reconnect with family and friends may highlight the need for a reunion. As you 'discover' new and interesting things from your family members, it may be wise to introduce these things to a larger audience. This process should not consume all your time because at some point you will want/need to begin your job search. Why not serve as the focal point to begin the planning process for the next or first family reunion? I am sure you will have family members who appreciate the fact you are being proactive and they do not have to be responsible for this event. Information you gather from talking with family members can be very valuable to ensure a successful reunion. You may actually use this premise to break the ice when initially reaching out to your family members in an attempt to reconnect with them... just a suggestion! Make sure you are available to help out even if you decide not to be the focal point for the family reunion.

Contact a family member or friend who lives in another city and/or state and arrange a trip to visit them. Your main reason for this trip is for a visit to catch up with them but you might be able to use this trip as a mini vacation (Chapter 2) and possibly start your job search in another locale. Catching up with your relative or friend in their location can provide you with a tour guide to local attractions and events. Planning this trip in advance would allow your relative or friend an opportunity to take off from work to spend even more quality time with you during your visit. Use their personal knowledge and familiarity with their city to help research activities and excursions for you if they cannot take time off while you are visiting. Make sure to let them know your travel plans to ensure you do not appear to be the relative who moves in and forgets to leave. Securing another job is on the horizon so do not let yourself get too comfortable while reconnecting with your friends and family.

Your time away from work also provides you with time to take the kids to amusement parks. You may want to get them out of school early one day or simply get up and go if they are on summer vacation. The planning for these outings should be less intense since you do not have to schedule the theme park activities around your work schedule. Use this time to enjoy spending a quality afternoon with the kids in an environment they would enjoy. Try putt-putt golf, video arcades or go-cart racing as alternatives if you do not live close to an amusement park. You may want to catch the new 3-D movie currently playing at the local movie theatre. The objective is to just get out of the house and enjoy the kids being kids. The need to rush through the park does not exist...enjoy!

I had the opportunity to experience some real quality time with my niece, Jayla during her spring break from 6th grade. We are very close but this was the first time we were able to spend an entire week just hanging out and looking for things to do. The suggestions I provide throughout this chapter were a major part of our visit together. We were able to experience a local Aviation museum together. I did not know if she would find this venue interesting but was extremely surprised by her interest in the aircraft on display. She asked some very insightful questions which I had a few answers for. The tools of war were things she seemed to gravitate to more than anything else. The old battle plans, uniforms, and small arms weapons on display provided us with hours of discussion and a very fun day at the museum.

The Georgia Aquarium in Atlanta, Georgia was another venue we visited during her spring vacation. Exploring the many sections of the aquarium allowed us to view sea life from all areas of the world. The display setup provided a good backdrop for us to take pictures to document our day at the aquarium which we shared with family and friends. A quick trip to the CNN Center gift shop allowed us to get some really good souvenirs to show we were there. Our next excursion to the Museum of Arts and Science was mentioned in Chapter 1. The art exhibits provided us with the chance to test our ability to judge artwork. We decided to assign our own scoring system to each piece of art and then we discussed why we liked or disliked a piece. We are not art critics but it was an activity we found a lot of enjoyment in. The museum has a small petting zoo and the handlers bring the animals out as part of their educational program with commentary. The animal handlers did an excellent job explaining the different traits of each animal and how they are treated at the museum. We even got a chance to go to a local golf driving range and hit golf balls. This was Jayla's first experience with golf and she seemed to enjoy the experience. I will have to reengage her interest in golf to see if we need to get her a set of golf clubs and get her on the course. The time we spent together probably would not have been possible if I was working during her spring break. We were able to get out and enjoy life together and have memories from this time to share.

The key in this process is to use your free time wisely and attempt to reconnect with family and friends. This simple gesture towards people in your life can be a great energy source to help you get through the time away from work. You may discover you have friends and family members who have been looking for a way to reconnect with you also. They always thought about picking up the phone to call but never got around to it for whatever reason. Take advantage of the opportunity you have to enjoy life with the people who mean the most to you and get reconnected.

RECONNECT
(ACTION PLAN)

Who would you like to reconnect with?

_____
_____
_____
_____
_____
_____
_____

What is the best way to reconnect with them?

_____
_____
_____
_____
_____
_____
_____

Where can you meet? (Coffee shop/book store/etc.)

_____
_____
_____
_____
_____
_____

Who would you like to visit if possible?

_____
_____
_____
_____
_____
_____

What activities can you include the kids in? (Amusement parks/putt-putt golf/etc.)

_____
_____
_____
_____
_____
_____

Chapter 4
TIME FOR A HOBBY

The extra time you have now can be used to get more involved with a hobby or start a new one. Your daily schedule completely belongs to you while you are away from work so delving into a hobby can provide a positive avenue for stress relief. How many times have you said you were going to learn to play chess, start fishing or take up golf? There were always more pressing things which kept you away from trying or finding a new hobby. This is your opportunity to actually get started exploring the hobby of your choosing.

An interesting thing I discovered with the extra time I have, my physical well-being has improved quite a bit. I am currently in the best shape of my life because I have unlimited time to work out and concentrate on staying fit. I still get up in the mornings and head to the gym at 5:30 a.m. to maintain a semblance of a normal daily routine. I can spend as much time on my exercise routine as I need to without worrying about making it to work on-time. I am a person who shunned the dreaded cardio machines and never truly took the time to do cardio. The cardio machines and running were things done as a last resort or only if necessary. I decided to use my extra time in the gym after hitting the weights to put a serious effort into a strenuous cardio workout routine. Hitting the elliptical machines or getting a nice uphill walk done on the treadmill did not seem to be as much torture as I had envisioned. I started to find myself enjoying this neglected part of my workouts after a few weeks into the program. The concept of doing cardio can be an enhancement to the weight training process. The resistance weight training I did added with the new cardio routines provided me with a positive start to each day. The gym can be a very good place to help relieve the stress you may experience being out of work. Why not make this process work for you?

You do not have to start out with a goal of competing in a body building contest, but use the gym to develop a form of self discipline and watch your physical well-being and psyche improve daily. Set some goals for yourself and put in the work needed to meet those goals. Most people make New Year's resolutions to work out more and to actually get back into the gym. Use this as an opportunity to make a life goal to get into better shape instead of a resolution and work towards this goal. The difference I see between a resolution and a goal is a resolution is made and can be broken or downgraded as needed. A written goal should be measureable to see what level of progress you have obtained to meet the goal. Try to set goals for the gym which you can measure and then begin in earnest to work towards those goals. Example: Bench press 250 pounds. Efforts should be focused on meeting this goal each time you train.

Keep track of everything you accomplish during your workouts to monitor your progress toward meeting this particular goal. Try to write down each exercise and repetition in your workout. This allows you to keep track of your progress and hopefully help avoid stagnation because you can see the exercises and repetitions you previously performed. The intent is to avoid doing the exact same workouts each week and keep your muscles confused so they can grow. This variety will bring a different level of intensity to your daily workout routines and help keep you from getting bored with the same daily routine.

Yoga is another physical activity I am able to devote quality time to with my time away from work. I tried yoga classes while in the Air Force stationed in Okinawa, Japan but it was just something to do during lunchtime and supplemented my weight training. Yoga was never a serious part of my workout routines in the past. I received several yoga DVDs as Christmas and birthday presents but never set aside time to devote to using them on a daily or weekly basis. The stretching and posing needed to master yoga was very intimidating to me at first. The amount of time I devoted in the past to my yoga DVDs was minimal at best. I laugh when I look back because I was not able to complete full routines without having to stop and catch my breath or the pain was unbearable for me. Getting into and holding a position was a major hurdle I had to overcome. The extra time available allowed me to put in more work with my yoga DVDs.

Baron Baptista and Rodney Yee are the two yoga instructors I have been following and the results have been positive so far. Routines I could barely make it through in the past became much easier for me because I could dedicate more time to them. The stretches and poses needed for each instructor provided me with a very good foundation towards a life of flexibility. Toes I had not touched in years suddenly came within range and were now easily accessible. This flexibility transferred over to the gym and helped my weight training workouts also. Most people are shocked when I tell them I use yoga DVDs but the results I see have made me a firm believer in the benefits of yoga exercises.

Check with your local gym or fitness center to see if they offer yoga classes and then take advantage of this opportunity. Gaining flexibility will help to enhance your outlook on life. Look at investing in yoga DVDs if your local gym or fitness center do not offer yoga classes. Find a yoga style and instructor to fit your current physical makeup and then get started. Yoga is a good way to start to change your physical well-being, improve your mental makeup and help get you prepared for a pending job search. Yoga and weight training are two of the hobbies I found additional time to devote to. These may not be the ideal hobbies for everyone so make sure you invest the time to discover things you truly want to do. Walking, running or golf may be the hobbies you have more interest in pursuing. The main point here is to find a hobby you like and enjoy the process of being active and engaged with your hobby.

Your reading interest is quite evident since you are viewing this particular book. Book clubs are a popular way to get back to reading basics. Identify family and friends who share a passion for reading and then get your book club started. The book club can also be a fun way for you to interact with your family and friends in a format you may have never thought of in the past. The club also provides a fun and rewarding experience for the members. Find ways to ensure all book club members have active inputs for the type books the club plans to review. Look to establish group guidelines the first time your group meets. This ensures everyone in the book club understand how the club plans to move forward. How often do you plan to meet? How will you choose the books for review? Where do you plan to meet? What time will your group meet? Who is in charge of the snacks? These are a few suggestions to get the process of establishing guidelines started for your book club. There will be others but at a minimum these will get you off the ground and running towards an effective book club.

Reading for your personal enjoyment will allow you to track your favorite author and get caught up on their latest offerings. Reading will also provide a mechanism to get your mind away from not working. Pick the style or genre that fits your personality or lifestyle best and dive into the reading process. You may gravitate to self-help books because of your current work situation. These type books may be the catalyst to provide the motivation you need to get back in the job market as soon as possible.

The key to your reading selection should be to provide some level of personal enjoyment and educational enlightenment. It is perfectly okay to enjoy the reading with a laugh or two. Autobiographies and classics may also provide a measure of reading enjoyment for you. Learning about leadership styles and personalities of some of our great leaders is an enjoyable process for me. Seeing how they developed and honed their style can enhance your leadership levels once you get back to work. Reading about a diverse group of leaders will allow you to pick and choose from their various leadership styles to incorporate into your own. Take the best from each you read about and develop a unique style of your own.

Books with a motivational angle may also be of value to you while you are away from work. These books can help with your mental energy level as you go through the process of enjoying a little time away from work. Use the motivational themes to redefine aspects in your personal and professional life. This is a time to reflect on past success or failure and identify ways you can improve in life. You may want to focus on ways to motivate yourself to get prepared for your pending job search. Your motivational focus could also be directed on ways to completely change your career goals and reinvent yourself. Create your personal 'vision' and then begin the process of working towards it. Daily quotes and affirmations are a positive way to ensure your mental makeup remains sharp and focused on the positive things life has to offer. Use these tools to find additional focus in life so you can move forward and get back to work on your terms.

Do not forget the topic of searching for a job while exploring your new found reading hobby. There are numerous books and articles available to help you prepare and then start your job search. Use this time to explore new techniques in the job search arena. Books on resume writing, cover letters and interviewing skills will help get you prepared to tackle the job market. It is always a good idea to get and stay current on job search techniques, so use this time to cultivate your reading hobby while also getting prepared to enter the world of looking for a job. Consider this type of reading as a personal investment into your near and distant future.

TIME FOR A HOBBY
(ACTION PLAN)

What things are you interested in?

_____
_____
_____
_____
_____
_____
_____

Would you like to explore a new hobby or spend more time on a current one?

_____
_____
_____
_____
_____
_____
_____

What have you always wanted to try but never had the time?

_____
_____
_____
_____
_____
_____

Who can you get to form a new book club?

_____
_____
_____
_____

What type books would the book club focus on?

_____
_____
_____
_____
_____
_____

What subjects are you personally interested in?

_____
_____
_____
_____
_____
_____
_____

CHAPTER 5
VOLUNTEER

The free time you have now can be put to very good use by volunteering your time and services in your community. We all state how we want to get involved and give back to the community. How many of us actually act on this concept? I have always been one to try to get involved but felt limited based on time available in the day. This was my ready-made excuse but the time away from work provided a perfect window for me to get as active as I should have been. You may find the personal satisfaction volunteering brings surpasses what you felt heading to work all those years. Look for things you may have been afraid to try while working and see if you like them. This is a chance to explore and find things you truly like doing. The benefits allow you to help out others while you enhance your daily satisfaction levels.

Volunteering serves a three-fold purpose in the grand scheme of things. The first purpose is it keeps the volunteer active. The second purpose is you can do some actual good in your local community. The third purpose is volunteering provides personal and professional networking opportunities. Why not use the skills you have from your work background to help out? The skills you have obtained in your professional life can be put to good use as a volunteer. The knowledge and passion you put into your working life can translate and prove to be valuable within an organization that relies on volunteer assistance to provide services in your local community.

Your leadership and management skills can help bring fresh and new ideas to whatever organization you decide to work with. Volunteers with training experience can help lead the community's efforts to get more people ready to pass their General Education Development (GED) exam. Volunteers with computer backgrounds can volunteer within the community to teach basic computer skills. Why not volunteer to help with the English as a Second Language (ESL) program at the local community or technical college? These are a few examples to highlight how skills you already have can help others and keep your skills sharp while you are away from work.

I decided to use my training and counseling background and volunteer with a local non-profit organization in Macon, Georgia. The first volunteer opportunity I had with this organization was as a participant in their elementary school reading program. This program brings local first grade students to the center and my volunteer task was to read to the students as they rotated to several learning stations throughout the facility. I believe I enjoyed this experience more than the kids! I was also surprised to see a majority of the first grade students were able to read many of the books for themselves. They were eager to hear the stories I selected for them but they were downright ecstatic when it was their turn to read. I quickly discovered their enjoyment of reading was more indicative of their desire to learn and show what they have learned. I was also happy to see the amount of involvement parents had helping these children with a desire to read. It was obvious which kids were active reading participants at home with parent involvement. All the kids were able to help read the stories at some level but there were quite a few who were very advanced readers to be in the first grade. The non-profit organization's reading program provided me with a way to give back and brought me a lot of enjoyment in the process.

My work within the reading program brought me into contact with other departments within this organization. My background was instrumental to the interest I received from the Director of Corporate University for a new, internal initiative started for staff employees. The Corporate University department was in the process of conducting Work Interest Assessments and implementing Individual Development Plans (IDP) for over 300 corporate and hourly employees within the non-profit organization. IDPs provide a planning process that identifies professional development needs and career objectives for employees. They felt my training and counseling background would be a perfect fit to help with this project. I saw this as another opportunity to use my skills to help others reach their personal and professional goals. This was also a way for me to stay active in a positive way and hone my skills within a different work environment. Keeping acquired skills sharp is a by-product of doing volunteer work. I was able to help the non-profit organization's staff with this project and continue to grow as a professional. It turned out to be a win-win situation for everyone involved.

    My time with this project consisted of classroom instruction to the staff and employees on the importance of understanding how Work Interest assessments can help with career selections. We worked with each employee to complete the assessments and then started the career exploration process. We quickly discovered most employees had a desire to explore their career options but never had an opportunity or access to accomplish this task. This was the first time they were provided with information to show them how to effectively plan their professional lives. The organization showed a high level of commitment and care to the employees by providing them with access to tools to explore their personal and professional interests.

Our next step after the training classes was to work with the staff and employees in a one-on-one setting to help them further explore their personal and professional options. Each employee used the information from the career exploration process to work with their supervisors to create an IDP. This document is used to help employees develop individual skills, enhance their office mission as well as set and achieve career goals. Setting and meeting career goals provides a set of measureable tasks each employee can view to gauge their progress on a daily basis. Their personal goals can also be incorporated within the framework of the IDP process. I am a firm believer in the importance of professional and personal goal setting. Written goals provide a marker so achievement and progress can be viewed. Adjustment can be made as needed but the goal remains viable and within reach.

Volunteering my time allowed me to help a group of people advance in their careers and provided me with work which I enjoyed. I was free to work on my own schedule and felt I was definitely making a difference.

The personal satisfaction this brought me was similar to personal satisfaction I got when I was working, maybe a little more because I could see the difference we were making with the staff. People who did not know me prior to attending our classes began to seek me out to let me know how their career exploration research was progressing. It became easier for them to approach me in the cafeteria and the hallway after we began to show them how the assessments can help them in the future. Many were eager to let me know they planned to sit down with me to get started with their new career plans. I enjoyed the positive effects we brought to their professional lives and how their immediate, professional outlooks were much brighter.

We were able to work with the department leaders and supervisors to ensure they understood their roles in the daily lives of their subordinates. Courses designed for them included Effective Leadership and Management, Becoming Management Material and Front Line Supervisors. The intent of their attendance in these courses was to ensure the managers and supervisors were in-tune with the needs of the people who worked for them. It would have been counterproductive to work with the employees to create career plans and IDPs and not work with the supervisors to ensure they understood the importance. The buy-in needed from the supervisors was stressed in each class we conducted with them. We discovered a majority of the supervisors never had formal training on what they were supposed to do or how to act. Many supervisors were promoted into the job in most cases and expected to perform at a high level. These courses provided them with the background needed to be successful in their current positions. They are now prepared to effectively work with their subordinates and help them succeed at work and in life. This part of the project was a revelation of sorts to me to highlight how training personnel to accomplish their job is an important and often times overlooked aspect in the work environment. Look for volunteer opportunities that you can see the impact you are making and see how your personal satisfaction levels go through the roof.

The volunteer work you do will allow you to network with a diverse group of people regardless of which organization(s) you decide to get associated with. Do not limit your options to only one organization if possible. I am a firm believer that you are always networking when you interact and meet new people. Your work style and personality can go a long way to help as you get out and meet the people working within the volunteer organization. The opportunity to meet the leaders of the volunteer organization and have daily interaction with them is a by-product of volunteering your services. You never have a second chance to make a first impression, so always make sure you carry yourself in an appropriate manner. Always ensure you present a positive, professional image and approach and ensure your actions compliment the mission of the organization you are working with. You may find yourself in contact with outside customers of the volunteer organization who may be able and willing to help you in the future. The networking contacts you make while performing volunteer activities may be able to help you in the future with your pending job search.

 Making your volunteer work stand out is a very good way to get noticed and potentially help lead to your next employment opportunity. Your volunteer activity may help with references or recommendations even if the organization you volunteer with does not have openings. You will have a documented work history with this organization if/when they have staff openings. Ensure you give yourself credit for this service by including your volunteer activities on your resume. This is work you have done so make sure it is documented properly. Never take volunteer work for granted; it can help open doors you may never have imagined. Seek out volunteer work you have a passion for while also targeting organizations you could see yourself actually working for. You may want to volunteer with multiple organizations so you do not limit your amount of professional exposure. Community involvement is another good reason to volunteer your time. Just stating a desire to be an active community participant is not enough. Actually leaving the house and finding ways to be involved can provide a valuable resource (you) to your community. Instead of complaining about things in your neighborhood, you can get involved and make a difference. Find something you are passionate about and look for ways to help your community.

Men can look to volunteer and mentor younger males who may not have a male figure in their lives. The time spent with these young men can go a long way towards showing them how to be a man. Having someone who takes the time to interact with them shows they have not been forgotten. The positive reinforcement mentoring can have on kids is a valuable by-product of your involvement.

Your involvement can be done through an organization which specializes in youth mentoring programs or you can step out and do it on your own. How many kids do you see at churches who do not have a male figure in their lives? The opportunities are there we just need to take action and get involved. This is not an attempt to pick on men because women can also get involved with kids who do not have female involvement in their lives. Step outside of your comfort zone and see if there are kids in your immediate surroundings who can benefit from an adult mentor in their lives.

There are many worthwhile organizations that would welcome the help from volunteers. I have always tried to seek out opportunities to help and give back to any community I have lived. While stationed in San Antonio, Texas with the Air Force I was active in the Big Brothers program. I worked with a local youth one-on-one as a Big Brother. The impact of this involvement was confined to this young man and his family but the overall Big Brothers program had a positive impact on several neighborhoods throughout San Antonio. I participated in an elementary school reading program while living in Biloxi, Mississippi. Once a week I worked with elementary school kids to provide support to their reading efforts. Most of these kids did not have anyone at home who could help them with their reading progression so reading mentors were extremely important to them. I am not saying anyone should mimic the community involvement activities I was involved with in the past but find your volunteer niche and get involved.

The time you have away from work can be used in many ways. Volunteering with organizations such as: Goodwill, Meals on Wheels, the Boys and Girls Club, the Salvation Army, mentoring programs, homeless shelters and soup kitchens can help you bridge the gap until you start working again. The contributions you make within your community help a larger audience and keep you active. Look to remain an active volunteer even when you go back to work; I am sure your community would welcome the help. Use this time to hone your skills, get personal satisfaction and network with as many people as you can. The good you do for others will help you in the long run...get out of the house and volunteer!

VOLUNTEER
(ACTION PLAN)

What local volunteer opportunities are available to you?

_____
_____
_____
_____
_____
_____
_____

Which of these opportunities are you interested in?

_____
_____
_____
_____
_____
_____
_____

What skills would you like to enhance with volunteer work?

_____
_____
_____
_____
_____
_____

Who are the points of contact for local volunteer opportunities you are interested in?

_____
_____
_____
_____
_____
_____

When can you start your volunteer activities?

_____
_____
_____
_____
_____
_____

How many hours can you volunteer?

Chapter 6
TEACH ONE, REACH ONE

The life experiences you have gained can be used to help others succeed in life. We discussed the concept of volunteering in Chapter 5. Finding an outlet to teach others life, computer or related skills can help you use your time away from work in a positive way. I am not saying everyone who is not working should rush out and become a teacher. I am also staying away from saying everyone should be able to teach others. The passion you have should already be on display before deciding to stand before any group and try to teach them a skill or task. This is a chance to get involved for those who have an interest and aptitude to teach and work with others.

How many times have you driven by a local community center and wondered what activities they provide? It may startle you to discover most activities in the community center are being provided by people who decided to give their time to help out. They discovered the urge to get involved in the center and to provide services for their neighbors. Your level of involvement will be determined by the amount of time you have available and the particular needs in your area. The skills you possess will also play a large role in deciding to work within the community center structure. Stop the car the next time you travel by the community center to see which programs they can use help with. Let the staff know you want to help out and see where you fit in their organization. Sign up to help kids in the after school reading program to influence their desire to become better readers. Work to help people with limited computer skills understand computer concepts and how to navigate around on the internet. There is a large population of people who have never touched a computer based on their specific life circumstances. They have heard people talk about things they could do on the computer but have never experienced it themselves. This may be an area to work with older people who would like to become computer savvy and never had anyone available to work with them on computer applications. You will have a huge impact on these people if you can get them comfortable working with and on a computer.

Non-profit organizations can provide you with multiple opportunities to teach skills to others. An important key when selecting a non-profit to work with will be how well their organizational values match up with your individual values. Organizations with missions that directly match your individual values will provide you with an avenue to teach some of those same values to other. The available courses within these organizations can range from teaching financial management concepts, life skills and parenting. The positive impact you have on people seeking services from the non-profit organization can provide them with the skills needed to be successful in life. Teaching opportunities within non-profit organizations benefits the local community and the organization you decide to work with.

Coaching youth sports is an excellent way to work with kids to ensure they learn the skills needed to be successful in their sport of choice. Think back to the influence a youth coach had on you during your early years when deciding if this is the type of teaching you would like to get involved with. The positive impact you can have with local youth in your community can help them as they continue to develop sport-related and life skills.

Ideally, the sport you decide to coach will be one you have some knowledge of. I played football, basketball, baseball and ran a little track while growing up in Florida. Sports provided me with a positive outlet and taught me valuable life lessons. These would be the sports I focus my coaching attention to because of my familiarity and interest in them. Other sports are still viable but it may be better to start with younger kids if you have limited knowledge in a particular sport.

Soccer has become a very popular sport in mainstream America but that does not mean it is right for everyone to coach. My soccer background is really non-existent but that does not stop me from being able to go out and kick the ball around. Limited sport specific knowledge does not equal limited ability to participate and help out. Learn the rules and strategies with the kids and ensure they have a good background in the sport as they progress towards the next age group level. Look to help the kids develop a foundation for the sport and then let them progress at their own pace. Suggest you research any sport you choose to ensure you know and understand the rules of the game so this information can be passed on to the kids. Teaching non-existent rules will do more harm to their learning of the game and potential enjoyment of their participation.

You may look to work your way into coaching youth sports by serving as an assistant coach to someone who has more experience in your chosen sport. Use this period as an apprenticeship to get a full understanding of the time required to accomplish your coaching duties. Make sure you are totally committed to this endeavor because there will be a lot of 'little' eyes watching your every move. Your coaching duties will put you in a role model position so make sure your actions reflect the self knowledge of this fact. The teachable moments you have with the kids can provide them with sport specific lessons, life related lessons or a combination of both. Take this position seriously because the influence you weld today can have long lasting impact with the kids into the future.

Teaching college courses as an adjunct faculty member is another excellent option to help fill the void away from your normal work activities. Teaching general education courses may be more appropriate for those who do not want to teach in an educational discipline similar to their earned degree. The Human Resources department for each school will list the instructor qualifications needed to teach at their institution. My educational background is in Psychology and Counseling. My focus to teach as an adjunct instructor centered on my educational background and desire to teach undergraduate Psychology courses. Your options to teach college courses have been expanded by the abundance of accredited on-line college programs. Most schools are enhancing their traditional course offerings with on-line courses to provide flexible options for their students. The decision to teach courses in-person or on-line will be determined by your current family lifestyle.

Teaching on-line courses will provide flexibility to complete teaching assignments from the comfort of your home while teaching in-person will require you to leave home and work in a physical classroom setting. Time will have to be set aside so you can fulfill your teaching obligations to include class preparation, assignment creation, grading papers and providing feedback to your students in a timely manner. Teaching college courses can provide a lot of personal satisfaction while still working to help others accomplish their educational and life goals.

An adjunct schedule provides a high level of flexibility which will allow the capability to still meet your personal and professional obligations. This flexibility allows you to get out and work a bit and still have time to work towards other life goals. The expertise you have gained throughout your lifetime can be used to help others continue to grow in their personal and professional lives. The salary you make as an Adjunct instructor may be the bridge you need during this transitional time in your life.

My personal experience as an adjunct instructor was gained in the on-line and classroom environments. My initial foray into the world of an adjunct instructor started with a nationally recognized on-line university. Responding to their on-line advertisement for adjunct faculty got the ball rolling for me to work with them.

Their in-depth hiring process required me to send in a resume, cover letter and all academic transcripts to see if my educational and professional background fit their current teaching needs. This first step of the hiring process was followed by an interview with their Human Resources department to further delve into my qualifications to match against their course and instructor requirements.

This step was followed by a training program to gauge perspective candidates' on-line interaction, tone, timeliness and ability to function effectively as an adjunct faculty member. Their training program was broken up into two-steps: core and specialized certification training. Each training module was two weeks in length and had to be done back to back before potential candidates could proceed forward with the hiring process. The training program's methodology ensures only the best qualified instructors get a chance to interact with the on-line students.

Core training provides a baseline for faculty candidates to ensure they can maneuver effectively through the series of interactive screens, folders and tasks required of an on-line instructor. The core training facilitators ensure all faculty candidates are well versed in the tasks required to be an on-line instructor before allowing them to move forward in the process. Faculty candidates are graded during this process and have to meet an established baseline during this two-week core training program. A grading rubric is provided to show things done well and specific areas for improvement. Faculty candidates who meet core training requirements move forward to the next training module. Faculty candidates who do not meet core training requirements are eliminated and cannot go forward into specialized training.

Specialized training provides a learning environment where faculty candidates actually facilitate training modules within a group of their peers. The faculty candidates are aligned with peers who would potentially teach in the same subject areas to provide a community approach to training and understanding requirements. Assignments in this training module directly related to course and daily interactions we could expect when working with a class or students individually. Scenarios presented during this module gave each faculty candidate an opportunity to learn and grow while also being evaluated for appropriateness of responses and daily interactions with peers and our facilitator. The challenge during specialized training was to ensure to meet stated on-line posting requirements while at the same time providing substantive material to keep each discussion moving forward. Things I initially thought were substantive required me to dig a little deeper to continue to move forward in this training module. A great part of specialized training was the interaction and support received from the other faculty candidates in my peer group. Everyone pulled together and shared knowledge to help complete this training so we could all move forward. Faculty candidates who do not meet specialized training requirements are eliminated and cannot go forward into the mentorship portion of the selecting process.

Faculty candidates who make it through specialized training are scheduled for a live mentorship as the final step in the hiring process. Each faculty candidate is assigned an experienced mentor who has been teaching in their specialty for awhile. The mentor is assigned to work with the candidates one-on-one as they facilitate a live course with 'real' students. This was an interesting process because my facilitator requirements were doubled during the mentorship: mentor forum and student forum. My mentor and I were required to communicate on a regular basis to ensure I followed all stated guidelines for adjunct faculty. I was able to ask my mentor for advice and procedural information to ensure I stayed on track for all assignments. An online forum was created which allowed my mentor and I to communicate in a private area separate from the classroom forum used to communicate with students. Faculty candidates were also required to interact with students in their assigned classroom forum which is where each course is facilitated. This dual forum mentorship required time management and organizational skills in order to complete successfully.

The dual approach in the mentorship process allows the mentor to provide feedback to each faculty candidate on ways to improve facilitation skills in the classroom forum. This was a valuable part of training because the feedback was direct and instantaneous which helps keep the learning environment active. Successful completion of the mentorship and recommendation from the mentor are required before faculty candidates can be hired to teach future courses with the school.

I was also able to work as an adjunct instructor in a traditional classroom environment. The process was not the same as experienced during the on-line teaching process. This was more of a traditional hiring process where my resume and transcripts were reviewed for a match against the teaching requirements posted. After interviewing with the Dean of the school, I was offered a position as an adjunct Psychology instructor teaching Introduction to Psychology courses for freshman students.

The challenge here was creating a syllabus from scratch to ensure coverage of the course text and provide the students with a well rounded academic experience. This entire process turned out to be a very enjoyable experience because I was able to work with students directly and take on the role of their 'mentor'. Watching them grow and expand their knowledge base was the most rewarding part of being in the classroom for me. Helping them understand the process of learning and how to apply course materials in their daily personal lives was a key factor in my wanting to step into the classroom. I was mildly surprised with the dedication of the students and their desire to learn. It was refreshing to see and a major motivating factor which will keep me in the classroom in some capacity.

Teaching can bring a lot of personal and professional satisfaction. It does not matter what level you decide to teach; your direct involvement can make the most difference in the lives of others. An interesting fact I noted from this experience is motivation to succeed has to come from within the students. Motivational tactics by any instructor can only go so far. The students will have to display the drive and willingness to work to meet their educational goals. A positive experience with an instructor who is there to help them meet or exceed their educational goals can go a long way towards helping them succeed. Do not take this step lightly because your involvement will put you in front of many eyes, some of whom may be very impressionable. Look to find your niche and if you have a passion to teach, get started today!

TEACH ONE, REACH ONE
(ACTION PLAN)

Do you have a passion to teach?

_____
_____
_____
_____
_____
_____
_____

What skills do you possess that you can teach to others?

_____
_____
_____
_____
_____
_____
_____

What local organizations can use your teaching skills?

_____
_____
_____
_____
_____
_____

What coaching opportunities are available in local youth sports leagues?

_____
_____
_____
_____

What colleges are in your local area? Do they have adjunct faculty positions available?

_____
_____
_____
_____
_____

Would teaching on-line courses fit your schedule better? Which schools are you interested in? What qualifications are needed to teach?

_____
_____
_____
_____
_____
_____
_____

Chapter 7
NETWORK, NETWORK AND NETWORK SOME MORE!

The free time you have away from work can be used in a multitude of ways. We have discussed how you can use this time to reconnect with family and friends. Simply taking time out to enjoy life without having to worry about the daily grind of work can be a very good diversion for you until you start working again. A major component you do not want to overlook is the impact of networking for your next career opportunity. Keep your eyes and ears open to the possibilities around you. Each time you meet someone regardless if you knew them previously is a chance for you to network into a better situation. These individuals may not be in a direct position to offer you a job or hire you, but they may have a friend or family member who may be in a position to help you get back into the work environment when you are ready. According to Ann Loyd, Director of Counseling at Macon State College, "You are always networking even if you do not know it". The impression you leave (good or bad) with the people you come in contact with can go a long way to determine how quickly you get back to work. The way you carry yourself, the way you dress, the way you interact with others are observable aspects in life which can affect your future career prospects.

This is a good time to dust off your personal contacts list and network with people who already know your work style and attitude. Let them know your current work situation and what type work you would like to do. Again, these people may not be in a position to hire you directly but they can 'drop' your name to someone who might. You do not have to overwhelm your personal contacts with a daily barrage but it is a good idea to engage these folks for help with your job search. Reconnecting with family and friends was a point of emphasis in Chapter 3; networking with them for leads towards your next career opportunity is a natural progression. You may also find your spouse's personal contacts valuable to your job search. Ensure you exhaust all possible links between friends and family members to create a large personal network to maximize your career search options. Establishing this network will put you in a position to get back to work when the time is right for you. This network can also keep you current on changing methodology and technology in your preferred field.

The professional contacts you have amassed over your working career can be very important to your networking endeavors. These are people who can directly vouch for your work history and performance. Make sure they know you are back on the market and have them on the lookout for possible openings in their organization or others they hear about. The professional contact can be very influential to your pending job search. A contact that has firsthand knowledge of your work experience, history and style may be an excellent source for a letter of recommendation or as a professional reference.

You want to make sure to identify someone who can speak professionally about the quality and quantity of your past work. This input can be very valuable to any future employers as they make hiring decisions for their organization. It is always a good idea to leave any work situation on a positive note. This may not always be possible but it would benefit you more than leaving a complete mess behind when you leave an organization. Leaving on a positive note helps you create a potential pool of professional contacts which can help you in the future as you change careers and/or organizations. 'Never burn bridges' is a mantra you can use throughout your professional life. Keeping these 'bridges' in working order provides you with a great source to reach out to for help at any point in your working life.

You may want to invite your contacts out to lunch or simply pick up the phone to discuss your current situation and seek their help. Try to remain in contact with people who can influence your job search even as you enjoy some time away from work. You do not want your professional contacts to get the perception you have completely disappeared from the working world. Maintaining contact can provide a valuable source of information to help you get back into the working environment when you are ready to pursue this avenue again. It is okay to enjoy some downtime but always be ready when opportunity presents itself to you.

Contacts you make from your volunteer activities are another excellent source to help you network your way to another career. Your efforts to get out of the house and make a difference in your community should bring you in contact with many people of influence. You realize you need to use outside sources to help with your job search efforts. Why not enlist the people you volunteer with to help in this process? Hopefully your volunteer work is done in an organization you have a definite passion or an affinity for their mission statement. This draw will put you in a position to work with the caliber and type of 'coworkers' you seek. Use your daily, weekly or monthly interaction with your volunteer community to let them see your high quality work standards. The passion and impact of your volunteer work can help establish your credibility within the volunteer organization and prove to be the catalyst to get you noticed in a positive way.

You can view volunteer opportunities as an informal work audition. You always want the work you perform to show a high level of professionalism. You should put maximum effort into any project you work on even if you are not being paid. This effort can go a long way to get you noticed by people in the organization who may be able to offer you work assignments or recommend you to another department or organization.

Networking is all about maximizing your visibility and viability to others. Someone who does not personally know you will have to see your abilities displayed before they can ascertain how these abilities can be used within their organization. Make it a point to meet as many people as you can while volunteering and let them know what projects you are working on. Never miss an opportunity to network while you are performing your volunteer activities. I am not saying to simply go up to everyone you meet and ask for a job but make sure they know who you are and what abilities you have 'in case' something comes open you may be interested in. Make sure your resume is up to date so you have it available when you get the request from one of your contacts. This will also let them know you are serious in your desire to work for their organization. You are always networking even if you do not know it so make sure you are prepared when it is time!

My volunteer work with the non-profit organization has provided me with an excellent environment to network in. My weekly contact with department directors, managers and hourly employees allow me to gauge the work environment from many different sets of eyes. They also get to see how I interact with them in their daily work activities. This interaction allows department directors and managers to see if I fit in with their staff and could potentially work there. In my five months volunteering with this organization, so far I have been asked if I was interested in full time work on three occasions. No promises were made but at least my work quality was effective enough to get me noticed within the organization. The networking I am able to do within the volunteer work environment is an added bonus to the good I am doing within the local community.

Networking can be done face to face or via the web in today's constantly moving world. The time you are in the gym working out puts you in contact with many people on a daily basis. Open yourself to the possibilities of simple communication with other gym patrons. Develop a friendly rapport over time and see if these new contacts can help you network yourself to a better position.

Leveraging technology can provide a faster way for you to network and make strong connections. There are several on-line networking sites which can help you in your pursuits. LINKEDIN and FACEBOOK are two popular sites which will allow you to connect with new and old contacts. There are numerous networking sites which you can use to stay connected. You may find using a combination of the sites listed below can go a long way to help your networking efforts:

BRIGHTFUSE – Allows the creation of a professional profile to highlight your professional background. www.brightfuse.com

FACEBOOK – One of the largest social networks. Allows users to join 'networks' organized by city, school, or company. Connect with 'friends' for personal and professional networking. www.facebook.com

LINKEDIN – Allows you to find, get introduced to and connect with professionals to help meet your professional goals. Get recommendations from people who are familiar with your work history. www.linkedin.com

PLAXO – Online address book and social networking service which provides automatic updating of contact information. www.plaxo.com

SPOKE – Business directory and social networking service used for professional networking. www.spoke.com

TWITTER – Social networking service allows users to send and receive messages: "tweets". Follow other users' activities via tweets or have users follow you.

Use these sites to identify people who may already work in an industry or organization you would like to be a part of. Your contacts on these sites can be the catalyst to help you get introductions and/or recommendations for job openings. Professional profiles should be created to ensure you are presenting the correct on-line image. First impressions count on the web also so you do not want an unprofessional picture or comment to derail your networking efforts before you begin.

An amazing experience I had involved working with a national educational speaker program to become certified to present their learning programs. This program is geared to provide educational presentations in high schools and colleges throughout the country. Each year the program administrators invite speakers from around the country to audition to present their programmed scripts in the different school levels. What an excellent opportunity to network with speakers of different levels and backgrounds from around the country? Everyone seemed to realize this was a target rich environment and made sure to ask for business

cards and contact information from different cohorts assembled. Many of us were just as happy to network with the other speakers as we were for the opportunity to work with this national educational program. Now I have contacts in California, New Jersey, Colorado and Ohio I would never have had a chance to meet without this opportunity. The plan is to stay in touch with these new contacts and see what the future may hold as far as working with them on other projects down the road. More people will be invited to participate each January and July so this provides a new crop of speakers to network with each year. A plan of action for events similar to this would include:
- Get a large quantity of business cards
- Have business cards available to pass out
- Make personal contacts and exchange business cards
- Follow-up with the new contacts you make
- Phone call
- Email
- Stay in contact for future business opportunities
- Network

You do not have to wait to be invited to a national program similar to the one I attended to begin establishing a network of peers. You can check locally for organizations which put you in contact with members in your community to begin establishing a solid network of contacts. Several local radio stations in Macon, Georgia put on a monthly 'Power Lunch' which is free to the first 100 listeners to sign up via their website. A free buffet lunch is provided followed by panel discussions on various topics affecting the local community. Starting a small business, community clean-up and saving our youth are a few of the topics we have discussed so far.

The energy and passion these topics create enhances the level of participation by those in attendance. The speakers who participate in this event are volunteering their time and expertise to help others succeed in life. This event provides an opportunity to network with local radio, television and print media personalities as well as other attendees from various educational and professional backgrounds. The diversity of the monthly participants makes this a very productive environment to hear experts speak on their topics, network and make new contacts.

Rotary, Toastmasters and professional organizations are other avenues you may pursue to ensure you are able to network with a larger audience. Check with each organization to see what their membership requirements are and then look to join if possible. You may not be able to attend each meeting but look for ways to get and stay involved to ensure you create a network suitable to help you in the future.

Do you have a car of your dreams? How often do you see this car after you think about it? Once your dream car is in your head it seems like you see this particular car everywhere you go. The car has always been there but once you decide it is the car of your dreams it is visible everywhere you turn. The opportunity to 'see' your dream car has always been there but you never let your mind focus on it until you declared it as your dream car. The opportunity to network has always been there for us all; we just need to be prepared to seize the networking opportunities when they present themselves to us. Do not allow valuable opportunities to get away from you any longer!

NETWORK, NETWORK AND NETWORK SOME MORE!
(ACTION PLAN)

List personal contacts you can network with.

_____
_____
_____
_____
_____
_____
_____

List professional contacts you can network with.

_____
_____
_____
_____
_____
_____
_____

Would social-networking be a better option for you? Which social-networking site is best for your situation? Would starting a BLOG help your networking efforts?

BRIGHTFUSE: _____
FACEBOOK: _____
LINKEDIN: _____
PLAXO: _____
SPOKE: _____
TWITTER: _____
BLOG: _____
Other: _____
Other: _____

**Do you have your own business cards?
Where can you get business cards printed?**

_____
_____
_____
_____
_____
_____
_____

What local organizations can you find networking opportunities?

Rotary club: _____

Toastmasters: _____

Lunch and Learn: _____

Book clubs: _____

Non-profit organizations: _____

Professional associations:

_____

_____

_____

_____

_____

_____

Other: _____

Other: _____

Chapter 8
GO BACK TO SCHOOL

The time you have away from work may prove to be the catalyst you need for motivation to go back to school. Enhancing your educational background may serve you well as the job market and technologies change daily. Being able to reinvent yourself and enhance your work skills through an educational program can make you very attractive to future employers. The path to finding a program of study to fit your life and future aspirations starts with you. Fully understanding your likes and dislikes will go a long way towards your successful selection of a program of study. This understanding will allow you to focus on things to fit your unique education, career and personal needs.

Simply saying you want to get back into school is not enough. Take the time to research schools and the programs of study each school offers. Selecting a school with full academic accreditation should also factor into your decision because this ensures their educational programs meet stringent academic requirements. An example: Southern Association of Colleges (SACS) accreditation identifies this association approves academic programs at a particular school and the school has to maintain requirements to keep this accreditation level.

Tuition rates, books and technology fees may also be considered in your process for selecting a school. Look at taking an interest inventory to help you get a better understanding of the things you like and dislike in life and your work environment. Interest inventories such as the Myers Briggs Type Indicator (MBTI) can be used to identify your personality type. (Please note: MBTI is one of many interest inventories available. Each school will identify their interest inventory of choice.) You will discover within each personality type, there are academic majors and professional occupations which correspond with that particular personality. This information gives you a working platform to begin the research process to identify what your program of study should be. The results you get from the interest inventory can be used with help from a school Career Counselor to select an appropriate program of study which fits your personality type and interest levels. The interest inventory helps prospective students to hone in on an appropriate program and eliminates the constant major changes seen with students who have not taken similar inventories. The goal will be to use your results to select the program which fits your interest levels and help get you off to a good start in school. The focus you gain by taking interest inventories can help lead to a successful completion of your program of study. Getting a handle on what you should major in can also help you set and maintain goals throughout your time in school. Simply saying 'I want to graduate' is not a very specific goal for anyone. Setting a goal to graduate in three years with a 3.75 GPA is very specific. The work you put in during your academic pursuits should be geared towards helping you reach the goals you set for yourself. You will be able to gauge your progress against measurable goals; adjustment can be made if needed. Write down your goals and try to keep them close by so you can refer back to them as a reminder of what you plan to accomplish. There is nothing wrong with making adjustments to your goals but make sure you use goal setting to help you get what you want out of your education. It is easier to make detours than to find out you have been pursuing something but did not have a plan or 'road map' to get to your desired location.

    I started my educational journey as a Business major then switched over to Sociology because that 'seemed' like a more interesting major. It felt like I was just taking classes to take them; which in fact is exactly what I was doing. My grades improved and I enjoyed learning more once I matched my interests with the appropriate program of study for me (Psychology). The school work I had to accomplish no longer seemed like work because I was studying things I was truly interested in. I still completed reading and research to meet course requirements but I found enjoyment in this process because I was learning what I wanted to learn instead of just trying to get through to get a degree.

The positive impact learning things I was truly interested in help transform me from an average student with no direction into a very good student with a purpose. This seems like an obvious pattern of progression but there are numerous people who struggle through school because they are not really interested in the courses they are required to take. The material may be dry to them or just not very interesting; their attitudes and most often grades suffer because of this lack of interest.

How many people do you know who are Business majors because someone told them they could make a lot of money in business? They may in fact be motivated to make a lot of money but have no interest in the courses needed to get this degree. Their effort to complete their coursework may suffer if they are not fully invested in their studies. Make sure you give yourself every opportunity to succeed in school. The courses you complete towards your degree can go a long way to help you gain employment if that is one of your goals.

For those who already hold a degree, this may be a good opportunity to go back to school to get a higher level academic degree, i.e., Masters or a Doctorate of Philosophy (PhD) or a degree in an entirely different discipline. You may find getting a higher degree will position you better for employment positions you were not able to reach previously in your field. This degree work will also show potential employers you have put in extra work to be successful within their company.

Going back to school to obtain certification, licensure or to learn an additional language may also prove beneficial for your professional outlook. Examples for this area include: certification (Information Technology), licensure (Real Estate), language (Spanish, French, others highly concentrated in your area). The additional coursework regardless if academic, certification, licensure or language training can provide you with skills which directly translate to higher level positions in your current or another organization. This may be the advantage you need to get your foot back in the door in the employment world. Displaying the ability to learn and apply course material highlight your capabilities to start and finish an objective you set out to meet.

The time I had away from work provided me with an opportunity to research and explore potential PhD programs for myself. Starting a doctorate program is something my mentor and I discussed in the past but I never fully engaged the process of obtaining school or program information. I was able to explore several schools and programs in-depth with a lot more free time on my hands.

My initial thought was to pursue a doctorate program that focused on counseling in an academic environment. My volunteer work with the non-profit organization helped me understand there is a much broader world out there which would be far more interesting to and for me. The employee development and training I did within the non-profit organization on a volunteer basis was something I enjoyed very much. The positive impact this work had on the employees could be viewed and felt instantly after their training sessions. Their professional and personal outlooks began to improve and I felt a lot of joy playing a role in this transformational process. I shared this information with friends and family and the consensus response was a doctorate program in Industrial/Organizational Psychology would fit me much better than a program in Counseling Studies. The ability to work in multiple work environments was a major draw for me to the Industrial/Organizational Psychology program.

Industrial/Organizational Psychology is a discipline that deepens knowledge of workplace and organizational behavior. This program also will provide a solid academic foundation for me working with adults in group and social settings. A major key for me selecting this program is it still keeps me aligned to pursue college and university faculty positions, training leadership positions and starting my own consulting firm. Other major work areas for the Industrial/Organizational Psychology program are:
- Selecting and placing employees
- Training and developing employees
- Appraising performance
- Developing organizations
- Enhancing employee quality of work life

The consulting firm is my ultimate goal once I complete my course work and dissertation requirements. Starting a business and setting my own agenda will be a challenge but one I am looking forward to. Starting and completing a PhD in Industrial/Organizational Psychology will enhance my skill set and allow me to pursue work opportunities which align better with my preferred professional path in life. This simple change in philosophy is a major step in the right direction for me! Can you think of ways this process can work for you?

Pursuing a degree in a new field may be necessary depending on the local job market and your current interests. Cross training within an organization is not a new concept; the premise is a person who cross trains can serve in multiple, interactive positions and has added value within the organizational framework of the company. An example of this process: someone working in customer service can also get certified to teach customer service skills to others. This person would now occupy two distinct and interactive positions in their organization. Their value quotient has also gone up! You may discover a new educational program may be helpful to make you more marketable to potential employers similar to cross training at work. The interest inventory results may prove helpful along with job trend information in your local area. Deciding to get a degree in another field is not going to help you if the field is nonexistent in your local area and you have no plans to relocate!

Your attempt should be to match your interest to a program of study which you can see future growth and a need. Use every available resource to help in your decision to pursue a degree in another discipline. You may consider using the Department of Labor Career Centers to help you project the potential growth of an occupation. Your school Career Center can also be used to look at occupations to see how much growth is projected in your local area, state or nationwide. The information you gather can be used to determine if getting a degree in another program of study is the best option for your particular life and work situation.

A growing national trend shows many people are pursuing educational programs at community and technical colleges. Programs can be completed at these institutions in two years or less which is an attractive draw for prospective students. The mission of these schools is normally tied to community, economic and educational development for the local municipalities. Programs can be completed towards associate degrees, diplomas and technical certificates. A majority of the programs are structured to help you complete multiple levels, i.e., occupational diploma courses can be applied towards associate degree programs. These same courses can also be used to receive specialized certificates in the same discipline. Each level builds up to the next level and provides a full spectrum educational portfolio to use towards your future employment endeavors.

You may find the CAREERSCOPE interest inventory helpful selecting your program of study in this environment. The schools will offer programs of study which are consistent with the types of industry in the local area. A location with a high concentration of aviation related industry will provide numerous programs of study to match the aviation industry's demand for employees in the area. Conversely, this environment can be very beneficial helping you select your program.

Understanding your likes and dislikes is just as important in these schools as it would be at a four year institution. Simply stating you want to be an Aircraft Maintenance Technician because of the prevalence of job opportunities in your area does not ensure you have the competencies to work in this field. Use the interest inventories to ensure you are selecting an appropriate program of study to fit your personal and work interest. This will help with your success level as you pursue your educational goals and ensure your selection process has a strong foundation.

GO BACK TO SCHOOL
(ACTION PLAN)

What impact would going back to school have on your life plans?

_____
_____
_____
_____
_____
_____
_____

What schools are in your local area?

_____
_____
_____
_____
_____
_____
_____

What programs of study are you interested in?

_____
_____
_____
_____
_____
_____
_____

Would taking an interest inventory help you decide on a program of study?

_____
_____
_____
_____
_____
_____
_____

What are your educational goals?

_____
_____
_____
_____
_____
_____
_____

Would obtaining certification, licensure or learning a language impact your life plans?

_____
_____
_____
_____
_____
_____
_____

Chapter 9
GET A MENTOR

Where there is no counsel, the people will fall;
But in the multitude of counselors there is safety.
(Proverbs 11:14)

Without counsel, plans go awry,
But in the multitude of counselors they are established.
(Proverbs 15:22)

We all need someone to guide us regardless of where we are in our individual life journey. Finding someone who can be your mentor can help with this transitional period in your life. Look for a mentor who displays the professional and personal values you would want to emulate. Aligning with this person provides you a sounding board with someone you have respect for. Picking a mentor should not be an exercise where you pick someone who will simply agree with whatever idea you throw out. The mentorship environment should provide you an opportunity to learn from your mentor and apply this knowledge in life.

You will need to be an active participant in the mentorship process. The mentorship concept provides you with a venue to grow on a professional and personal level so you will need to ensure your involvement is sufficient to enable the growth you seek. The time you spend with your mentor may be limited so make the most of the time set aside by your mentor. Show them you understand their time is valuable and you want to maximize your time together. You may view this process as a partnership between you and your mentor. You both have something invested in this process: getting you to meet or exceed your life and professional goals.

Ideas and suggestions given to you by your mentor should be acted upon in a timely manner. There will be times when you will take advice from your mentor and immediately put that advice in action. Your mentor will be available to help you plan a process but you still have ownership of the outcomes. A mentor cannot make you take actions; they can only point you in the right direction with guidance on how you can handle a task. Guidance you take no action on, falls squarely on you in this process. Remember, you have to take responsibility for your actions to ensure the mentorship is successful. Your mentor can help you gauge progress towards a planned conclusion but you will need to ensure you put in the necessary work to reach your stated personal and professional goals.

Why are goals important in this process? Goals can provide a map to show you direction and guide your actions. Goals can also help you gain personal or professional focus and can be measured over time. Simply saying you want to get something accomplished is not by definition a goal. The difference between a dream and a goal is the written word. Dreams are things you state without having a plan to work for or towards them. Think of all the resolutions most of us make every year in January. We have good intentions but the effort comes up short without a more concrete way to work towards our resolutions. Normally, these resolutions have been either changed or forgotten by April and we vow to make the same changes 'next year'. This cycle seems to repeat itself every year for most of us.

Effective goals are written down so you can periodically refer to them to gauge your progress towards meeting these stated goals. The goals you create need to be complete and focused towards different aspects in your life such as educational, professional or health goals. Make sure the goal you set is something you really want to accomplish. Your goals need to be consistent with your personal and professional values. There will be times when family or friend influence may come into play when you are trying to work on your goals. Try to ensure the goals you create are your own; without undue influence from family or friends. Their intentions may be to help you with your goals but their input may lead you away from the things which are most important to and for you.

Make your goals positive instead of negative. How many times have you talked yourself out of something because you had negative thoughts about the process? Thinking positively in everyday life will help you grow as a person. The concept of 'positive self-talk' is not new; give it a try to see how it can impact your life. Talk your way through the process of meeting or exceeding your goals. Identify what you 'want' to accomplish when you begin setting your goals, not what you want to leave behind. A positive goal can lead you to positive results. Make your goals high enough to meet your stated purpose and then put in the work to meet them. Again, simply saying you want to do something is not really a goal.

We make statements all the time but creating your personal and professional goals should be more than just talk. Write your goals down and then put in the work to accomplish them. It is okay to make adjustments as needed but the main thing you want to accomplish is to reach your ultimate goals. Use this process to help get started:

- **Categorize your goals**
  - Personal
  - Professional
  - Others as needed
- **Write down your goals**
  - This creates a road map for your success
  - Review goals frequently – quick status check
  - Change does not mean failure - you may need to make adjustments
  - Visualize your completed goal
  - Creates positive self-talk
  - Keeps focus on working towards the goal
- **Make sure your daily decisions focus on meeting or exceeding your goals**

A mentor is also someone who can set a positive example and provide motivation either through words or actions. Look for someone who projects an image which fits the direction you want to go in. For example, someone who has already obtained success in the field you would like to go in would potentially be an excellent choice for a mentor. I say potentially because if you do not have a personal relationship with this person, you would need to get to know them to ensure they are the right person to mentor you. Simply looking at how a person dresses or talks is not a good way to select a mentor. Take time to really get to know this person to see if a mentorship with them is appropriate. Let them know you are looking for a mentor and why a mentorship would be a helpful process at this point in your life. Make sure you share with them how and why you selected them to be your mentor. Recurring meetings with your mentor will allow you time to discuss your plans and see how much progress you have made towards meeting your goals.

My mentor has played a huge part in my drive to succeed in life. She made a very simple suggestion to me one day, "Make sure you stay in contact with me when you move on to bigger and better things". At the time, I said I would but did not fully understand the depth this statement would have on me over time. By acknowledging she knew I could do even more, she provided me with the motivation to seek out the things that were important to me. Living my life took on a whole new perspective once I received my motivational talk from my mentor. She did not provide my inner drive but her statement, because it came from someone I admire and respect gave me extra confidence I could succeed in any endeavor. I mentioned the national speaker program earlier in Chapter 7. The networking I was able to accomplish during this event was amazing. Want to guess who gave me the motivation to compete with speakers from across America? If you guessed my mentor, you would be 100 percent correct! I have not mentioned her name but just so everyone who reads this knows; it is Ann Loyd. She has provided me with inspiration and guidance to tackle projects I never imagined I would. This book and several chapters have materialized because of comments she has made to me over the time we have spent talking about life.

I recently started putting into practice the concept of regular meetings with my mentor. I make sure to get on her calendar on a day and time that fits her schedule. Never forget your mentor is there to help you out but meeting with you takes time from their normal activities. It helps to have flexibility when trying to setup times to meet. This time allows us to catch up on things that are happening in both of our lives. We then get down to business and work on gauging progress towards my written goals. This is the perfect time to ask for your mentor's opinion on projects or tasks you are thinking about adding to your list. Use your meetings as a way to seek 'counsel' to ensure you are heading in the right direction on projects you have on tap.

Provide your mentor with enough details so they can help you formulate a plan of action or even to enlist additional help for you. A very good thing about my mentor is she is well connected in our community and if she does not have direct knowledge of something, she will put me in contact with someone who does. Remember when we talked about networking in Chapter 7? Well this type of give and take between mentor and mentee is a form of networking. My mentor is available to help me meet my goals but she also is a good source to put me in contact with the right people whenever needed. So as you can see, a mentor can provide valuable help to you as you move forward in life. The partnership you establish with a mentor can impact you in many positive ways. The 'counsel' mentioned at the beginning of this chapter can be gained within the mentorship process. How can a mentor help you with your personal journey?

A wise man will hear and increase learning,
And a man of understanding will attain wise counsel.
(Proverbs 1:5)

GET A MENTOR
(ACTION PLAN)

List the benefits of having a mentor.

_____
_____
_____
_____
_____
_____
_____
_____

Create a list of potential mentors.

_____
_____
_____
_____
_____
_____
_____
_____

**What is the best way to contact potential mentors?
Who can introduce you to potential mentors?**

_____
_____
_____
_____
_____
_____
_____

How often would you like to meet with your mentor?

_____
_____
_____
_____
_____
_____
_____

What are your goals for the mentorship?

_____
_____
_____
_____
_____
_____
_____

How will you gauge your progress during the mentorship?

_____
_____
_____
_____
_____
_____
_____

Chapter 10
LIVE LIFE; GET OUT OF THE HOUSE!

*If I didn't define myself for myself, I would
be crunched into other people's fantasies
for me and eaten alive*
(Audre Lorde)

Remember the life scenario I posed to you in Chapter 1? 'Yesterday you were working; today you do not have a job! What in the world are you going to do with yourself?' Hopefully you have made the decision to live life and not let life live you. In the past, the person with control over your paycheck had a certain level of control over you. Why not take back some of this control and decide to work in an environment of your choice? Your emotional and mental well being may be at stake. Losing or actually choosing to leave your job may be the break in life you have been looking for. You may discover you like the idea of having more freedom to pick and choose your path in life. Explore the possibilities and see which direction your compass points when you encounter the fork in the road on your journey through life. You own the process and can choose the direction you take in life.

Reassess your life priorities and use this time to discover what is really important in your life. The decisions you make right now can provide the springboard you need to live the life you have always wanted. Losing or leaving a job is a major event in anyone's life; what you do with yourself will help determine how you deal with this event. Do you live as a victim of circumstance or do you take action and control of your life? These are serious questions for a serious and pivotal time in your life. This is not the time to mourn 'what' has happened but a time for action within your individual lives.

An easy way to view this period is as a brand new chapter in your book of life. The blank pages in this new chapter are ready for you to fill in with new life events and experiences. A good friend of mine has a little saying he likes to use when working to help motivate people to reach their goals in life; "You can't hit a home run if you don't swing". This is a very simple statement but it sums up quite a bit for anyone trying to make a change in their personal and work life situations. The simplicity of this statement has done quite a bit to keep me moving forward on several projects I have recently undertaken. The option to be an active participate in your life journey is there for you to seize! The journey is going to happen regardless of your level of participation. Are you willing to live a little? What are the things that motivate you in life? Use this time away from work to locate your motivational factors and ensure your future endeavors can help you get there. Eliminate any doubt you may have and set your course towards the things you want to accomplish in life. The positive self-talk concept can really be used to help you as you move towards the things you really want. Use the internal drive that you displayed in your previous work environments to help find your motivation and start to live your dreams. A motivated life can be a wonderful way to reenter the workforce and get you back on course towards a good life and work balance.

The normal 'preconditioned' thought process would lead you to an immediate search for new career opportunities. If your current life situation determines this is an appropriate process for you and your family, then you need to get busy exploring your potential career opportunities. Let me repeat that so there is no misunderstanding of the point being made here: if you need to get back to work right away, then that should be your priority at this point in your life. Give yourself a few days to relax and unwind before you jump back into the hustle and bustle of a work environment.

Individuals with a little more life flexibility should seriously consider enjoying their time away from work to indulge in activities they may have put off because the timing was never right. This is not an overarching endorsement to forget the important things in your life, but an attempt to highlight the possibilities that we as a whole are always overlooking. Take the necessary time needed to evaluate your position in life to see what option you need to pursue in the near term. Create a list of things you have always wanted to do or achieve and prioritize them to highlight their importance to you. Now comes the really hard part! Actually get out of the house and start accomplishing the things you have written down. The whole process sounds simple as you read this, but guess what? It can be just that simple.

How you start this process is completely up to you. You may find yourself going through your list of phone numbers and addresses to identify friends and family you have not talked to in awhile. Your purpose here will be for you to see who you need to reconnect with in the near future. Do not feel bad if you discover it has been a long time since you communicated with many of the people in your address book. This can be attributed to your mind state of putting all your energy and effort into your past work situation. View this exercise as a new beginning which will allow you to rediscover how much your friends and family mean to you. Make sure these personal and professional connections remain a major part of your life 'after' you get back into the working world. The thing you want to avoid from happening is going back to ignoring these people all over again after you go back to work. You have signaled they have importance to you while you are away from your work comfort zone; do not ignore these relationships you have rebuilt during this timeframe.

Use your time away from work as an opportunity to 'find' yourself. This sounds like a funny concept when reading the last sentence out loud but the value you get out of this process may be eye opening. What are some of the things you like about your life? What things do you dislike? Being truthful with yourself when answering these questions may provide valuable insight into how you move forward from here. Things you like can still be incorporated into your future endeavors be it at work, home or at play. How cool would it be to actually do things in life you enjoy in every aspect of your daily life?

Things you dislike would be identified during this process and you will have to make a decision to ensure those things are not a part of your daily life anymore. This may not be a simple endeavor but it can get you to start understanding what your life priorities are and how they are determined. For instance, if you write down that you dislike putting in 12 hours days at work because it takes away from your family time; then focus your new job search on careers where you have more control of your work hours. If you write down you dislike traveling for work, then your search would lead you to eliminate careers with a huge travel factor involved.

Do not put yourself in a 'funk' and start hiding out in the house. Make a promise to get out of the house regardless of which fork in the road you decide to explore on your personal journey. There are many activities you can explore during this timeframe in your life, so get out there and live life! Try to establish some type of 'self' routine where you have a daily event to look forward to. This could be as simple as picking up the kids from school or having lunch with a friend. Getting dressed and leaving the house can have a positive effect on your daily disposition. This simple act provides a 'purpose' to your daily activities and can boost your mental makeup. You can also use leaving the house as a part of your new daily routine. Run errands, go to the library or volunteer; just get out of the house and enjoy life! So, what have you decided? Are you going to live life, or let life live you?

Our visions begin with our desires
(Audre Lorde)

LIVE LIFE; GET OUT OF THE HOUSE!
(Action Plan)

1. **Start a journal. Write down ways you can Live Life.**
   a._____
   b._____
   c._____
   d._____
   e._____

2. **How can you take control of your life situation?**
   a._____
   b._____
   c._____
   d._____
   e._____

3. **What are the things that motivate you in life?**
   a._____
   b._____
   c._____
   d._____
   e._____

4. What are your priorities?

a._____

b._____

c._____

d._____

e._____

5. What have you always wanted to do but never pursued?

a._____

b._____

c._____

d._____

e._____

ACKNOWLEDGEMENTS

Renee, my wife, for having the patience to allow me to work on this book and find different ways to figure out the question: What Now?

Velora, my mom, for your love and belief all goals are obtainable with a little hard work and dedication.

Jayla, my niece, for allowing me to hang out with you on your spring break and come up with some ideas to use in this book. Thanks for showing your uncle a new way to view life!

Phillip, my brother, for always believing I can get things accomplished and continue to improve in life daily.

Ann Loyd, my mentor, for your friendship and guidance. I am amazed by the amount of information I get from you each time we sit down and talk! My motivation comes from within but you have been very instrumental in helping me as I continue to look for ways to 'Live Life'. What's our next project?

Kim Gibbs, my friend, for editing and making sure my intended thoughts were translated into print for this project. I hope the next book project will be a complete collaboration so we can bring Kim & Calvin to the world! Get your topics together!

Phillip Jr. and Alexis, my nephew and niece, for your support.

LaSandra Simmons, my friend, for providing a 'fresh' set of eyes and your experiences to this project.

Reco and Kiana, my brother and niece, for your support.

Denny, my father-in-law, for providing an analytical eye and life experiences to help guide me in this process.

Cristina, Taryn, Liza, and Ken, my Detroit family for your support.

You the reader, you took a chance and picked this book to read. I hope you have found new ways to take control and live life. Be on the lookout for additional titles in the future!

NOTES

Notes

NOTES

Notes

Notes

www.ingramcontent.com/pod-product-compliance
Lightning Source LLC
Chambersburg PA
CBHW070642050426
42451CB00008B/263